How Did We
Find Out About
Superconductivity?

The "HOW DID WE FIND OUT . . . ?" SERIES
by Isaac Asimov

How Did We Find Out About Superconductivity?

Isaac Asimov

Illustrated by Erika Kors

Walker and Company
New York

Dedicated to

Madeline Greenberg, a beautiful 1987 addition to the human species

Text copyright 1988 by Isaac Asimov
Illustrations copyright 1988 by Erica Kors

First published in the United States of America in 1988 by the Walker Publishing Company, Inc.

Published simultaneously in Canada by Thomas Allen & Sons Canada, Limited, Markham, Ontario.

Library of Congress Cataloging-in-Publication Data

Asimov, Isaac, 1920–
    How did we find out about about superconductivity? / by Isaac Asimov ; illustrated by Erika Kors.
        p. cm.—(The How did we find out—? series)
        Includes index.
        Summary: Discusses the history of the development of superconductive materials and explores the problem of finding materials that are superconductive at higher temperatures.
    ISBN 0-8027-6776-1   ISBN 0-8027-6778-8 (reinf.)
        1. Superconductivity—Juvenile literature.
[1. Superconductivity.]   I. Kors, Erika W., ill.   II. Title
III. Series: Asimov, Isaac, 1920–   How did we find out—series.
QC612.S8A75   1988
537.6'23—dc19   87-24142
                                                                        CIP
                                                                        AC

Printed in the United States of America

10 9 8 7 6 5 4 3

Contents

1
Measuring Temperature

Scientists are trained to ask questions. Why does water change to ice when the temperature goes down? How cold is the coldest temperature? Why does dry ice behave differently from regular ice? In laboratories and in the field, researchers experiment to move step by step toward an answer.

Sometimes several scientists in different parts of the world are working on the same question. Sometimes new scientists pick up experiments where older ones stopped.

While they are looking for one answer, scientists sometimes discover something else quite new and unexpected. They find an answer to a question they weren't even asking. These surprises are a special reward of working in science.

When researchers tried to find out all about temperature, an exciting event happened—they discovered *superconductivity*. This discovery could change our everyday world.

Let's follow the footsteps of the searchers to that surprise—a way of transferring energy without losing any of it to the drag of wires or conduits.

We all know that it is warmer by day than it is by night. It is warmer in the summer than it is in the winter.

Some things—like boiling water or a match flame —are very hot, hot enough to damage us. A piece of dry ice is very cold, cold enough to damage us.

For that reason, we don't want to test how hot or how cold something is by touching it. If it were too hot or too cold we would be in pain. Even if it were just pleasantly warm or pleasantly cool, it would be very hard to tell by touch alone just how warm or cool it might be.

We need an instrument to do the measuring, something that is more reliable than our touch.

As it happens, things undergo certain changes as they grow hotter or cooler. For instance, most objects expand slightly, growing a little larger, as they warm up. They also contract slightly, growing a little smaller, as they cool down.

Such changes are very small and we don't usually notice them. Suppose, though, that we have a hollow bulb that is filled with the liquid metal *mercury* (MER-kyuh-ree). Attached to the bulb is a glass tube with a long, thin hollow inside it. Within the hollow is nothing at all, not even air. In other words, it contains a *vacuum* (VAK-yoo-um), which is from a Latin word meaning "empty."

Suppose, next, that the mercury is warmed. It expands very slightly, so that some of it is forced up into the thin tube that is attached to the bulb. The more mercury is warmed, the more it expands and the higher the column climbs. If the mercury is cooled, it contracts and the column falls.

From the height of the mercury column, you can tell how cool or warm the mercury is, and therefore how cool or warm the air or water around it is. Such an instrument is called a *thermometer* (ther-MOM-uh-ter), from Greek words meaning "to measure heat." The height of the mercury column tells us the *temperature* (TEM-per-uh-choor).

The first mercury thermometer of this kind was made in 1714 by a Dutch scientist, Gabriel Daniel Fahrenheit (FAH-ren-hite, 1686–1736). In order to be able to measure temperature in numbers, Fahrenheit marked off the glass tube containing the mercury column into equal divisions and numbered them—1, 2, 3, and so on. Each division is called a *degree* (dih-GREE), from Latin words meaning "step."

But where do you start counting from? One way of getting a low temperature to start from is to chop up ice and mix it with water. If you put the bulb of a thermometer into such a mixture, the level of the mercury will mark the *freezing point* of water, and that level can be labeled zero.

Fahrenheit felt the freezing point of water wasn't cold enough. So he added salt to the water. Salt water freezes at a lower temperature than pure water does. He added enough salt to get the freezing point as low as he could and marked off that level of the mercury column as zero.

He then marked off a higher level where pure

water froze and a much higher level where pure water boiled. He divided the column between the freezing point and the boiling point into 180 equal sections and continued that down to his zero mark.

By this *Fahrenheit scale*, the freezing point of water was at the 32 mark and the boiling point was at the 212 mark. So we say that the freezing point of water is "32 degrees Fahrenheit," while the boiling point of water is "212 degrees Fahrenheit." We can abbreviate this as "32° F." and "212° F." (The little circle means "degrees.")

Using this scale, the normal temperature of the human body is 98.6° F. When a person is sick, the temperature rises a bit to 100° F. and higher. We say you then have a "fever."

The Fahrenheit scale is not really very convenient. The freezing point and the boiling point of water are not expressed as simple numbers. In 1742 a Swedish scientist, Anders Celsius (SEL-see-us, 1701–1744), suggested a different scale. He set the freezing point of water at 0 and the boiling point at 100.

Now we can say that the freezing point of water is "0 degrees Celsius," or "0° C," and the boiling point of water is "100 degrees Celsius," or "100° C." Body temperature would then be 37° C.

This *Celsius scale* proved so popular that it is now used in every nation but one. The exception is the United States, which uses the Fahrenheit scale. Even in the United States, scientists use only the Celsius scale.

In this book, I will use the Celsius scale too, but I will put the Fahrenheit scale alongside in parentheses for a while.

Anders Celsius

The mercury thermometer is one way of measuring temperatures, but it is not the only way. Other ways must be used to measure temperatures that are so high that mercury boils, or that are so low that mercury freezes. We won't bother with the other ways in this book, though.

How high can temperatures go? The air around us heats up under the summer sun. The highest air temperature ever measured on Earth came on September 13, 1922, in what is now the nation of Libya. The temperature was then 58° C. (136° F.) in the shade.

The Sun shines down on the hotter parts of the Earth for about twelve hours at a time, and the wind can bring in cooler air. On the Moon, the Sun shines down for two weeks at a time, and there is no air and so no cooling breezes. On the Moon, temperatures can reach as high as 117° C. (243° F.). This is higher than the boiling point of water.

Temperatures are hotter at the center of a large body than they are at the surface. The temperature at Earth's center is about 6000° C. (12,000° F.). At the center of Jupiter, the temperature may be as high as 54,000° C. (97,000° F.), and at the center of the Sun it may be as high as 15,000,000° C. (27,000,000° F.)

Stars that are larger than the Sun are hotter, too. Some stars may have central temperatures in the thousands of millions of degrees.

When the universe was first formed, and when all its material was squashed into a tiny little object smaller than an atom, its temperature may have been in the trillions of trillions of trillions of degrees. It seems, then, there is no limit to how high temperatures may go, or how hot something might be.

Let's try the other direction and consider how cold things might become.

Temperatures on Earth can go many degrees below zero C. If a temperature is ten degrees below zero C., we can say it is "ten Celsius degrees below freezing," but it is much more convenient to say it is "$-10°$ C." The minus sign shows it is below zero.

The coldest place on Earth is the continent of Antarctica, which is at the South Pole. Soviet scientists have established a base at a place in Antarctica that is farthest from the ocean, so that it gets colder there than anywhere else. On July 22, 1983, they measured a temperature of $-89.2°$ C. ($-128.6°$ F.). That is the coldest temperature ever measured on Earth.

On the Moon, where there is no air to bring in warmth from elsewhere, it can get even colder. The night on the Moon is two weeks long, and the temperature drops through all that time. By the end of the long night it can be as low as $-127°$ C. ($-261°$ F.).

Planets that are very far from the Sun have even lower temperatures. Pluto, the farthest planet, may have a temperature at its surface as low as $-218°$ C. ($-360°$ F.).

Does this mean there is no limit to how cold an object may be? Is there no limit to how low temperatures can get?

Oddly enough, the answer is that there *is* a limit. Although temperatures can go up to any height, it seems, they cannot fall to any depth. There is a temperature that is as cold as it can possibly be, and nothing can ever be colder than that.

An ordinary zero of temperature is nothing more than a convenient figure. It was convenient for Celsius to set the freezing point of water as 0° C., but temperatures can go lower than that. Fahrenheit thought it convenient to set the freezing point of salty water as 0° F., but temperatures can go lower than that, too.

Even if we set zero at the coldest temperature ever measured in Antarctica, or on the Moon, or on Pluto, temperatures can go lower than that, too. If, however, we set zero at the lowest temperature it is ever possible to have, then that is a *real* zero.

When we have a zero that is truly the lowest temperature there can be, so that there is never anything lower, we call that *absolute zero*.

The question is, though: How did scientists get the idea that there was such a thing as an absolute zero?

2
Finding the Lowest Temperature

THE FIRST PERSON to get a notion that absolute zero might exist was a French scientist named Guillaume Amontons (ghee-OME a-mon-TON, 1663–1705).

Amontons was very interested in ways of measuring temperature, but he lived before Fahrenheit had invented the mercury thermometer. He tried, instead, to measure temperature by considering how air expanded as it grew warmer and contracted as it grew colder. Such an "air thermometer" is not very good, but Amontons grew more and more interested in this expansion and contraction.

He noticed that as air grew cooler, it seemed to contract at a steady rate. What's more, he noticed that other kinds of gases also contracted at the same

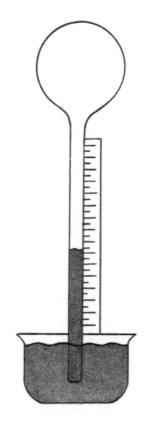

Galileo's air thermometer

steady rate. It seemed to him that if air, or any other gas, kept getting cooler, its volume would get less and less and less until, finally, that volume would drop to zero.

Since you can't very well expect a gas to shrink to a volume of less than zero, it would mean that temperature could only go down so far. Once it reached the point where gases had zero volume, there would be an absolute zero and nothing colder could exist.

Amontons made this discovery in 1699, but it didn't seem to impress anyone very much, and his work was forgotten for a long time.

Then, in 1787, another French scientist, Jacques Alexandre Charles (SHAHRL, 1746–1823), also studied the volume changes of gases with temperature. Charles had a great advantage over Amontons, for by his time mercury thermometers had been invented.

If Charles began with air at 0° C. and let it cool to −1° C., he found that it contracted by about 1/270th of its volume. For each further degree that it dropped, it contracted by another 1/270th of its volume at 0° C. Other gases acted the same way.

In other words, suppose you start with 270 cubic inches of air at 0° C. If the temperature drops to −1° C., the volume drops to 269 cubic inches. At −2° C. it is 268 cubic inches, at −3° C. it is 267, and so on. By the time you got down to −270° C. or thereabouts, the air volume would be 0 cubic inches and that would be absolute zero.

Charles didn't write up his discoveries and publish them so that other scientists could see what he had

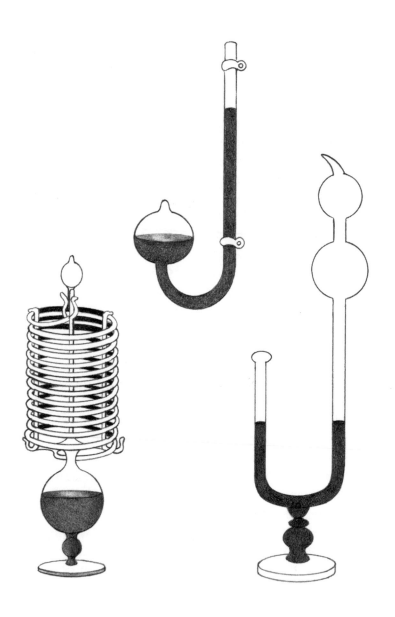

17th-century thermometer

done. Maybe he thought the idea of having an absolute zero was too weird to talk about openly. Still, he kept private notes, so we know about his ideas.

Then, in 1802, yet another French scientist, Joseph Louis Gay-Lussac (GAY-lyoo-SAK, 1778–1850), did the same kind of work. He got the same results Charles had, but he published them. That made many scientists begin to think about absolute zero and try to figure out just exactly what the temperature of absolute zero might be.

Nowadays, scientists have determined that absolute zero is at $-273.15°$ C. ($-459.67°$ F.).

There is a catch, though, when it comes to working out the temperature of absolute zero by measuring the decrease in volume of gases. After all, gases don't stay gases as the temperature drops. At least, some gases don't.

Water may be a gas at temperatures over $100°$ C. ($212°$ F.), but if you cool it to that temperature it liquefies. Alcohol is a gas that liquefies at $78.4°$ C. ($173.1°$ F.). Ether liquefies at $34.6°$ C. ($94.3°$ F.), and a gas called butane liquefies at $-0.5°$ C. ($31.1°$ F.).

Once a gas becomes a liquid, it continues to contract as it gets cooler, but at a much smaller rate than a gas would.

In Gay-Lussac's time, air and certain other gases remained gases, even at the lowest temperatures that scientists could then reach. Still, it made sense to suppose that at still lower temperatures, those gases too would turn liquid and then shrink very slowly indeed as they were further cooled. In fact, liquids, when

Joseph Gay-Lussac

very cold, might stop shrinking in volume altogether. In that case, volumes would never become zero and temperatures might drop far below −273.15° so that there might be no such thing as an absolute zero.

In 1848, a British scientist, William Thomson (1824–1907), considered this problem. (Later in his life, Thomson was given a title by the British government and was named Baron Kelvin. For that reason, he is generally known as Lord Kelvin. Sometimes, even when speaking of the work he did before he got the title, writers refer to him as Lord Kelvin.)

Lord Kelvin reasoned that all substances were made up of tiny atoms that usually combined into small groups known as *molecules.* In gases, the molecules moved freely about. In liquids and solids, they remained in place but moved rapidly back and forth in that place.

Whether the molecules moved freely or just trembled in place, the motion meant that they possessed energy. The higher the temperature and the hotter the substance, the more rapidly the molecules moved, and the more energy they had. The lower the temperature and the colder the substance, the more slowly the atoms or molecules moved, and the less energy they had. This proved true of all substances, whether they were gases, liquids, or solids.

Kelvin showed that what counted was the energy in a substance, not its volume. At absolute zero, the energy of *any* substance dropped to zero and couldn't drop any further. So absolute zero *did* exist at −273.15° , regardless of whether gases all became liquids at low temperatures or not.

gas

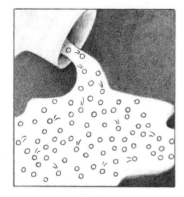

liquid

solid

Behavior of molecules

Lord Kelvin

In 1851, Kelvin pointed out that it made sense to measure all temperatures from absolute zero and to move upward by Celsius degrees. Such a temperature scale is the *absolute scale* or the *Kelvin scale*, named in his honor.

Absolute zero is "zero degrees Kelvin," or "0° K." Since absolute zero is 273.15 degrees below the freezing point of water, water freezes at a temperature 273.15 degrees above absolute zero, or at 273.15° K. To change Celsius temperatures to Kelvin temperatures, you just add 273.15 to the Celsius figure. Water boils at 100° C., and since $100 + 273.15 = 373.15$, water boils at 373.15° K.

For the rest of the book, I will use the Kelvin scale, with the Celsius scale in parentheses.

3
Turning Gases into Liquids

ONCE GAY-LUSSAC LED scientists to thinking about absolute zero, they began to wonder whether they could liquefy air and other gases at temperatures higher than absolute zero. To do that they might have to cool the gases to very low temperatures, even if not quite to absolute zero.

But in Gay-Lussac's time they had no way of reaching the necessary low temperatures. They could get really cold temperatures only if they went to Siberia in the winter (or, much later, to Antarctica). Even then, the lowest temperature in Antarctica is still 184° K., or almost two hundred degrees above absolute zero. That might not be enough to liquefy some gases.

In 1823 an English scientist, Michael Faraday (1791–1867), thought of another way. If a gas is put under pressure, that forces the molecules closer together, which increases its tendency to turn into a liquid. If you put a gas under pressure combined with low temperatures, it might turn into a liquid more easily than with low temperatures only.

Faraday began with a strong tube of thick glass. He put at its bottom a quantity of a chemical that gave off chlorine gas when it was heated. He melted the other end of the tube shut and heated the middle so that he could bend it into a boomerang shape.

Next he put the end with the chemical into hot water and the other end into ice water. At the heated end, chlorine gas was formed in greater and greater quantities. This produced greater and greater pressures. Finally the great pressure, together with the cold from the ice water, produced liquid chlorine at the cold end.

Chlorine liquefies without pressure at a temperature of $238.6°$ K. ($-34.5°$ C.). It could easily be made to liquefy in a Siberian winter. But cold plus pressure could be used to liquefy other gases that ordinarily liquefy at still lower temperatures.

Besides, this gave scientists a new way of getting low temperatures. Suppose a gas is liquefied under pressure and its container is surrounded with cork or some other material that will keep outside heat from getting in. The container is then opened a bit so the liquid starts to boil and to turn into a gas. For the gas to form, the molecules of the liquid must pull apart. That involves energy. The energy can only come

Michael Faraday

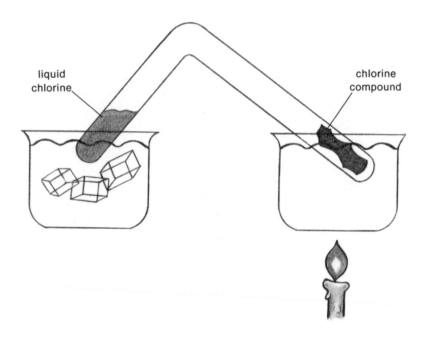

liquid
chlorine

chlorine
compound

Faraday's liquification of chlorine

from the liquid itself, so as the liquid evaporates, it quickly gets very cold.

In 1835 a French chemist, C.S.A. Thilorier (tih-lore-YAY), started with the gas carbon dioxide (dy-OCK-side) and liquefied it by Faraday's method. He used metal tubes, which are stronger than glass ones. After he had prepared quite a bit of liquid carbon dioxide, he let some of it evaporate. It cooled down further and became solid carbon dioxide.

Solid carbon dioxide looks like ice, but it doesn't melt into a liquid. A block of solid carbon dioxide turns slowly into gas without passing through the liquid form. For that reason, it is called "dry ice." It turns into a gas at a temperature of 194.6° K. (−78.5° C.).

Dry ice can be chopped up and added to liquid ether, which doesn't freeze till very low temperatures are reached. The dry ice cools the ether, which slowly evaporates, getting still colder as a result. A mixture of dry ice and ether can reach a temperature as low as 163° K. (−110° C.). This is far colder than any temperature even Antarctica can produce.

Now, instead of producing a gas at one end of a tube and cooling the other end in ice water, you could cool the other end in a dry ice–ether mixture. This meant you could easily liquefy many gases that couldn't have been liquefied before.

In fact, by the 1860s, there were only four known gases that couldn't be liquefied. They were *oxygen* (OCK-sih-jen) and *nitrogen* (NY-truh-gen), the two gases that make up air; *carbon monoxide* (mon-OCK-side), a poisonous gas found in automobile exhaust; and *hydrogen* (HY-druh-jen), the lightest of all gases.

Four more gases were discovered by the end of the 1800s that couldn't be liquefied by dry ice–ether cooling either. They were *fluorine* (FLAW-reen), *argon* (AHR-gon), neon (NEE-on), and *helium* (HEE-lee-um).

The difficulty in liquefying these gases was explained in 1869 by an Irish scientist, Thomas Andrews (1813–1885). He found that the higher the temperature of a gas, the greater the pressure required to liquefy it — and the pressure required rose more quickly than the temperature did. Above a certain "critical temperature," *no amount of pressure* would liquefy a gas. The eight gases that couldn't be liquefied had critical temperatures *below* 163° K. Before they could be liquefied they had to be made colder than a dry ice–ether mixture.

In 1852, however, Lord Kelvin (who was still only William Thomson) and a friend, the English scientist James Prescott Joule (jool, 1818–1889), showed that making a liquid evaporate into a gas was not the only way of forcing a drop in temperature.

Suppose you put pressure on a gas, squeeze it into a small container, and then cool it as much as you can. If you allow this compressed gas to expand, that too takes energy, which is absorbed from the gas itself. The temperature drops quickly.

This is called the "Joule-Thomson effect."

In 1877 a French physicist, Louis Paul Cailletet (kah-yuh-TAY, 1832–1913), compressed oxygen as much as he could. Then he cooled the compressed oxygen to as low a temperature as possible and let it expand. Its temperature dropped, and eventually he managed to get a fog of small droplets of liquid oxygen. He did the same for nitrogen and carbon monoxide and got droplets of liquid there, too.

The technique was improved, and by 1883 scientists were getting these liquid gases in quantity. In fact, twelve years later, a German chemist, Carl von Linde (LIN-duh, 1842–1934), managed to work out a way to make liquid air (composed of oxygen and nitrogen) in such large quantities that it became cheap enough to use in industry.

By 1895, it was possible to liquefy five of the eight difficult gases. Here are the temperatures at which these five turn liquid.

Oxygen	90.17° K	−182.98° C.
Argon	87.28° K.	−185.87° C.
Fluorine	85.01° K.	−188.14° C.
Carbon monoxide	81.70° K.	−191.45° C.
Nitrogen	77.35° K.	−195.80° C.

Scientists had now produced temperatures within seventy-seven degrees of absolute zero, but there were still three gases they couldn't liquefy: neon, hydrogen, and helium. The Joule-Thomson effect didn't seem to work for these three.

Meantime, in 1873, a Dutch scientist, Johannes Diderik van der Waals (van-der-VALS, 1837–1923), had studied gases with particular care and explained the difficulty. From the results he got, it became clear that, for these three gases, the Joule-Thomson effect only worked below certain temperatures.

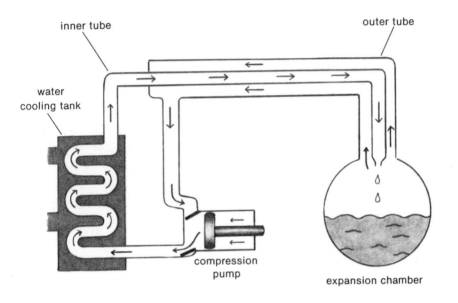

inner tube

outer tube

water
cooling tank

compression
pump

expansion chamber

Apparatus for liquifying air

For almost all gases, the temperature at which the Joule-Thomson effect started to work was quite high. At ordinary temperatures it would serve to cool almost any gas.

For hydrogen, however, the Joule-Thomson effect would only work at temperatures below 190° K. (−83° C.). This meant that hydrogen had to be

James Dewar

cooled to a temperature colder than the coldest Antarctica winter before it could be further cooled by letting it expand. The Scottish chemist James Dewar (DYOO-er, 1842–1923), was the first to take this into account.

He began by making large quantities of liquid nitrogen, with a temperature of 77° K. (−196° C.).

This was far below the temperature at which the Joule-Thomson effect would begin to work with hydrogen. He took a quantity of hydrogen, compressed it in a strong container, and dipped the container into the liquid nitrogen.

The compressed hydrogen cooled down to liquid nitrogen temperatures and *then* Dewar allowed it to expand. The expansion cooled it further, and in 1895 he finally got liquid hydrogen.

Hydrogen liquefies at $20.38°$ K. $(-252.77°$ C.). The technique that worked to produce liquid hydrogen could also be used to produce liquid neon, for neon liquefies at a slightly higher temperature than hydrogen does; neon liquefies at $27.05°$ K. $(-246.10°$ C.).

Dewar also had worked out a way of keeping very cold liquids from evaporating too quickly. He did this by preparing containers with double walls. In between the walls there was a vacuum.

Heat can be transferred into or out of a container by passing through the material of the walls. But in this double-walled container, there was nothing between the walls that the heat could pass through. Heat can also be carried by air currents, but there were no air currents between the walls.

Finally, heat can radiate, producing tiny waves of energy that *could* pass through a vacuum. Dewar took care of that by lining the walls of the container with smooth, shiny metal. The metal reflected most of the radiation and wouldn't let it pass through. This meant that hardly any heat at all could pass through the container walls.

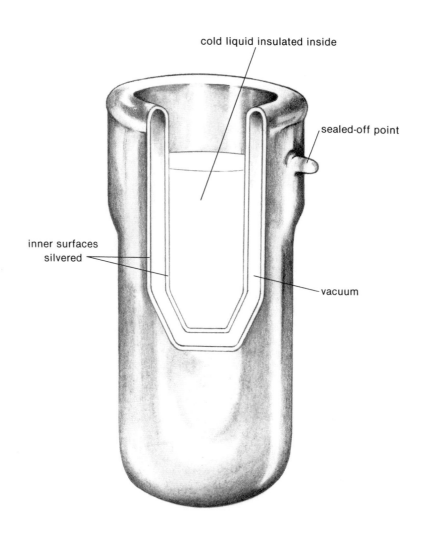

cold liquid insulated inside

sealed-off point

inner surfaces silvered

vacuum

Cross section of Dewar flask

If very cold liquids are put in such a container, so little heat will get in that the liquids remain cold for a long time and hardly evaporate. Such a container is called a "Dewar flask."

People use these flasks at home and call them "thermos bottles." Outfitted with corks and caps, they can be used to keep water or other drinks cold. They can also be used to keep coffee or soup hot.

Dewar placed some liquid hydrogen in one of his flasks and let it evaporate. The evaporation used up heat that had to come from the liquid hydrogen itself, since almost no heat came from the outside. As it evaporated, the liquid hydrogen cooled further. In 1899, Dewar was able to freeze it and form solid hydrogen. Hydrogen freezes at a temperature of $13.95°$ K. $(-159.20°$ C.).

And yet, even at a temperature within fourteen degrees of absolute zero, helium remained a gas. It was the only gas that had not been liquefied as the 1900s began.

4
The Helium Struggle

HELIUM IS MADE up of the most stable atoms that exist. The helium atom is so stable that any change in it is bound to make the atom less stable. For that reason, it won't combine with any other atoms. It won't even combine with other helium atoms, so that helium gas is always made up of single atoms. On the other hand, hydrogen, oxygen, nitrogen, and fluorine are made up of atoms that combine in pairs. So we speak of hydrogen, oxygen, nitrogen, and fluorine *molecules.*

Helium atoms are so stable that they do not come together long enough to form a liquid unless the temperature is very, very cold. In this deep cold, the helium atoms can hardly move at all.

A Dutch scientist, Heike Kamerlingh Onnes (KAM-er-ling OH-nes, 1853–1926), decided to tackle

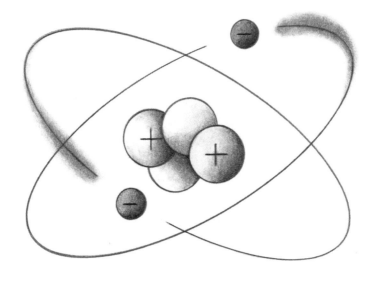

Helium atom

the problem of liquefying helium. He designed a special laboratory where scientists worked only with very low temperatures. It was the first laboratory of the kind ever set up.

Kamerlingh Onnes then compressed helium tightly and let it cool in a bath of liquid hydrogen.

Heike Kamerlingh Onnes

Once the helium was as cold as the liquid hydrogen, the Joule-Thomson effect would work. He then allowed the very cold compressed helium to expand so that it grew colder still. Finally, in 1908, he produced liquid helium. The last gas had now been liquefied!

The temperature at which helium becomes liquid is only 4.21° K. (−268.94° C.).

To keep this extremely cold liquid helium from evaporating too quickly, as much heat must be kept out as possible. So the container of liquid helium was kept in a larger container full of liquid hydrogen, which was kept in a still larger container full of liquid air.

In this way, Kamerlingh Onnes kept his helium liquid long enough to experiment with it. He wanted to do one more thing, and that was to freeze it and produce solid helium. He managed to cool the helium by letting some of it evaporate quickly. In this way, he got the temperature as low as 0.83° K. (−272.32° C.), but the helium stayed liquid. When the scientist died, on February 21, 1926, he still had not managed to freeze helium.

We now know that it is impossible to freeze helium just by lowering its temperature. At absolute zero, there is still a very tiny bit of energy left after all. This energy cannot be removed, so that absolute zero remains the lowest temperature we can reach. That little bit of unremovable energy is just enough to keep helium atoms from settling down into a solid arrangement.

A few months after Kamerlingh Onnes died, however, a student of his, the Dutch physicist Willem Hendrik Keesom (KAY-sum, 1876–1956), decided to try a combination of high pressure *and* low temperature, as Faraday had done with chlorine almost exactly a century earlier.

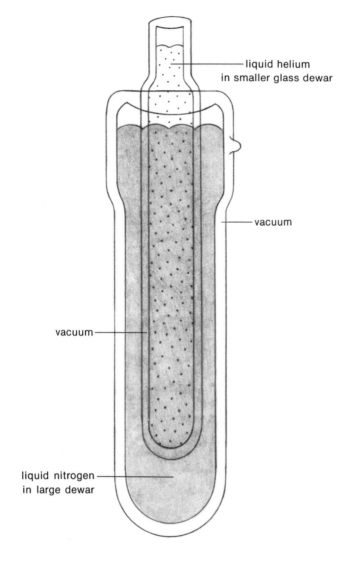

liquid helium
in smaller glass dewar

vacuum

vacuum

liquid nitrogen
in large dewar

A double dewar keeps heat in

This worked. When Keesom put liquid helium under 25 atmospheres of pressure, he found that he could obtain solid helium at 1.0° K. He even managed to lower liquid helium temperatures to 0.4° K.

Even though scientists had now managed to liquefy and solidify all known substances, they were not satisfied. There is always the desire to reach a limit—to reach the North Pole or the South Pole, or to climb Mount Everest, or to rocket to the Moon.

In this case, though, it was impossible to reach the limit. In 1906, just two years before helium was finally liquefied, a German scientist, Walther Hermann Nernst (1864–1941), showed that one could only approach absolute zero, but never quite reach it.

Suppose you start at 4° K., the temperature at which helium turns liquid. It would take a certain amount of effort to remove half the energy and reduce the temperature to 2° K. It would take about the same amount of effort to remove half the energy that was still left and get down to 1° K. It would then take the same effort to get down to 0.5° K., then to 0.25° K. More and more effort will continue to lower the temperature, but in smaller and smaller steps, and you would never get all the way to 0° K.

Still, scientists would like to approach absolute zero as closely as possible, and evaporation did not seem to get them lower than 0.4° K.

In 1926, the Dutch scientist Peter Joseph Wilhelm Debye (dih-BY, 1884–1966), had an idea. There are some molecules that are sensitive to the pull of a magnet. A magnet will force them all to line up in

Early 20th-century low-temperature laboratory

the same direction. Suppose this magnetized material is cooled by liquid helium down to 0.4° K., the lowest temperature that can be reached by evaporation, and then the magnet is removed.

All the magnetized molecules can now point any which way, and they do. But it takes energy for them to fall out of line in that way, and the only place they can get the energy is from the liquid helium that surrounds them. This means the temperature of the liquid helium will drop.

In 1933 an American scientist, William Francis Giauque (JEE-oke, 1895–1982), tried this method, and it worked. He got the liquid helium down to 0.25° K., only a quarter of a degree above absolute zero.

Dutch scientists, on hearing of this, also used magnetized molecules, and before the end of the year they had reached a temperature of 0.0185° K., only 1/54th of a degree above absolute zero.

Other devices to remove tiny scraps of heat from very cold liquid helium were also tried, and now temperatures as low as 0.00002° K.—only 1/50,000th of a degree above absolute zero — have been reached. But absolute zero itself has never been obtained and, it seems, never will be.

Getting down to these low temperatures proved interesting, because scientists learned things they had never known before.

In 1928, for instance, Keesom had discovered that at 2.2° K. helium changed from an ordinary liquid, "helium I," with properties like all other liquids, to a

Portable liquid-helium storage tank

new kind of liquid, "helium II," which had properties no other liquid seemed to have.

Helium II, for instance, was a "superfluid" that could move through the smallest holes without any friction. Containers that were airtight might not be helium II–tight.

Helium II also conducted heat perfectly. Any heat that was added to it spread over the entire liquid at once. No hot spots developed, so that helium II didn't boil by forming bubbles but merely by peeling off the uppermost layer of atoms.

Then, too, helium consists of two varieties of atoms, called "helium-4" and "helium-3." Helium-4 is the common type of helium. Only one helium atom out of a million is helium-3.

It is really helium-4 that liquefies at $4.21°$ K., and it is helium-4 that turns into helium II at $2.2°$ K.

In the 1940s scientists were at last able to separate the occasional helium-3 atom out of helium and produce a gas that was just about all helium-3.

Helium-3 atoms are only three-fourths as heavy as helium-4 atoms. It is even easier for helium-3 atoms to fly away from each other than it is for helium-4 to do so. That means that helium-3 should liquefy at an even lower temperature than helium-4.

In 1949, scientists found that helium-3 liquefies at $3.2°$ K., a full degree below the point that helium-4 does.

Helium-3 did not show any signs of turning into a helium-II form of liquid. It was cooled to lower and lower temperatures in order to see if such a form of helium-3 existed. Not until 1972 was helium-3 turned

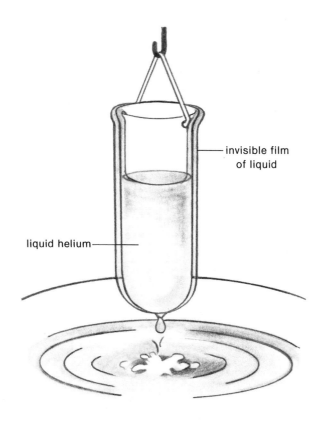

invisible film
of liquid

liquid helium

Helium-II "Superfluid"
climbing up and out of its container

into a helium-II liquid—at a temperature of 0.0025° K., only 1/400th of a degree above absolute zero.

Helium-4 and helium-3 are the only substances that form this strange kind of liquid. No other substance remains liquid at a low enough temperature.

Scientists like the Soviet physicist Peter Leonidovich Kapitsa (KA-pyit-seh, b. 1894) have eagerly studied this strange material in order to understand more about the structure and properties of atoms.

5
Super-
conductivity

ONE DISCOVERY MADE while studying liquid helium now looks as though it might prove to be of enormous importance in everyday life. It came about this way.

Once liquid helium had been produced, scientists were able, for the first time, to study various properties of matter at very low temperatures.

For instance, when electricity passes through a wire, it meets up with a certain *resistance*. It has to force its way past the atoms in the wire, and this uses up some energy, which turns into heat. As a result, the wire grows hot and only some of the electricity manages to get through.

If the wire is cooled to begin with, the atoms in it move about less speedily and don't interfere with the electric current as much. In other words, the resistance decreases. Most scientists assumed that resistance would continue to fall, little by little, as the temperature of the wire fell, and would finally reach zero at a temperature of absolute zero.

This seemed to be true when temperatures were reduced all the way to that of liquid hydrogen. In 1911, Kamerlingh Onnes, who had first liquefied helium three years before, decided to try to check this matter of electrical resistance further by using liquid helium temperatures. He expected no surprises, but he got an enormous one.

Kamerlingh Onnes was studying frozen mercury, which carries electricity with not too much resistance, and which shows even less resistance at liquid-hydrogen temperatures. At 4.21° K., the liquefying point of helium, the resistance of mercury was just about where scientists expected it to be.

But as Kamerlingh Onnes dropped the temperature further, he found that at 4.12° K. the resistance suddenly dropped to *zero*. Below that temperature, mercury conducted an electric current *perfectly*. There was no conversion of any of the electricity to heat, because there was no resistance. Because electrical conductivity under these conditions was perfect, the phenomenon was called *superconductivity*.

Scientists had never expected that there would be zero resistance at temperatures above absolute zero. It wasn't till 1973 that an American scientist, John Bardeen (b. 1908) offered a reasonable explanation. Still, explanation or not, mystery or not, scientists were anxious to know whether only mercury acted in this way or whether other metals did too.

They quickly discovered that other metals *did* show superconductivity. A few didn't, but that might be only because they weren't tested at temperatures quite low enough.

For instance, the metal hafnium (HAF-nee-um) can be superconductive, but only if it is cooled to a temperature of 0.35° K. or below. Only a few metals became superconductive at temperatures higher than mercury did. Lead, for instance, becomes superconductive at 7.22° K. An electric current set up in a lead ring that was kept in liquid helium continued to circle round and round for two and a half *years* without losing any electric current in all that time.

The metal with the highest superconductive temperature is technetium (tek-NEE-she-um), a radioactive metal that doesn't exist in nature but can be made in the laboratory. It becomes superconductive at 11.2° K.

Superconductivity might have important uses. Electricity is always being conducted from the generators where it is produced to the homes, offices, and factories where it is used. Up to 15 percent of all the electricity conducted here and there is lost as heat. This amounts to many billions of dollars.

Suppose electricity could be carried through superconductive wires. None of it would be lost and billions of dollars would be saved. But if the highest superconductive metal will work only at a temperature lower than 11.2° K., we must surround all our wires with liquid helium. Nothing else is cold enough. Liquid hydrogen, the next coldest liquid, freezes at 14° K. and, unless allowed to evaporate continuously, will be at a temperature of 20° K.

Helium, however, is very rare, and keeping it

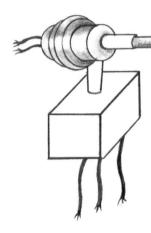

Equipment for testing sample materials for superconductivity

The sample of ceramic being tested is clamped (far right) on a long holder or probe (across top of drawing, above). Wires from the sample go through the probe to the terminal at left to record results.

The middle drawing on the right is a close-up of the sample chip. The picture in the circle shows the testing wires attached to the sample chip.

The whole probe is immersed in a refrigerated container, or superthermos, and electric current is sent through the wires. The test measures the rate at which the electric current travels through the ceramic sample at various temperatures.

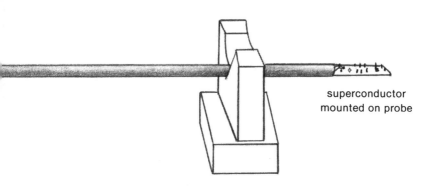

superconductor
mounted on probe

close-up of end of probe

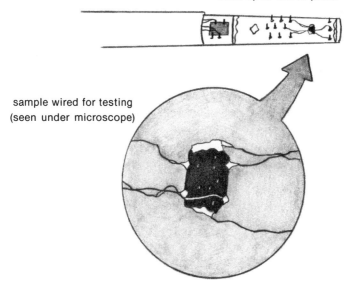

sample wired for testing
(seen under microscope)

53

liquid is extremely difficult. It would cost far more money to keep all the conducting wires cold enough for superconductivity than we could possibly save by doing so.

What is needed, then, is something that is superconductive at higher temperatures. Since no pure metal will do, perhaps a mixture of different metals, an *alloy*, might be found.

Scientists began to test every alloy they could get their hands on. About fourteen hundred of them were found to be superconductive at low temperatures, but always at temperatures that were too low to be practical.

Not till 1968 was an alloy found that would be superconductive at liquid-hydrogen temperatures. An alloy of the metals niobium (NY-oh-bee-um), aluminum (a-LOO-mih-num), and germanium (jer-MAY-nee-um) was found to become superconductive at 21° K. In 1984, an alloy of niobium and germanium reached the mark at 24° K.

Liquid hydrogen is more common than liquid helium and is easier to keep liquid, but still not easy enough. Besides, liquid helium is at least utterly safe, while liquid hydrogen can burn. It can also produce vapors of hydrogen gas that can explode. Using liquid hydrogen all over the nation in order to transport electricity would not only be an unbearable expense, it might give rise to great disasters.

In three quarters of a century, nothing warmer than 24° K. had been found for superconductivity. The situation seemed hopeless.

And then came another big surprise, one as big as the original discovery of superconductivity.

In Germany, scientists tried something new. Instead of testing metals that were pure or mixed (the usual conductors of electricity), they began to test combinations of metals with oxygen, or *oxides* (OKS-ides). These oxide mixtures are claylike substances called *ceramics* (seh-RAM-iks), from a Greek word meaning "clay." The dishes we eat out of are usually made of ceramic materials.

The first word of this came in the fall of 1986, when it was announced that a mixture of oxides of lanthanum (LAN-thuh-num), barium (BA-ree-um), and copper (KOP-per) had turned superconductive at 28° K.

This wasn't much of an improvement, of course, but suddenly everyone was testing all kinds of ceramic mixtures and the mark was soon bettered. Before the end of the year a ceramic was reported that was superconductive at 40° K.—provided it was placed under huge pressure. Another laboratory, however, quickly announced a ceramic that was superconductive at 36° K., even with no pressure at all.

It didn't stop there. In 1987, a ceramic was developed that was superconductive at 90° K. Such a ceramic would be superconductive at liquid nitrogen temperatures. Liquid nitrogen is much more common than liquid hydrogen, is easier to keep liquid, and is almost as safe as liquid helium.

Even there discoveries haven't stopped. In May 1987 came a report of a ceramic that might turn superconductive at a temperature of 225° K. (−48° C.). This would mean superconductivity at dry ice temperatures.

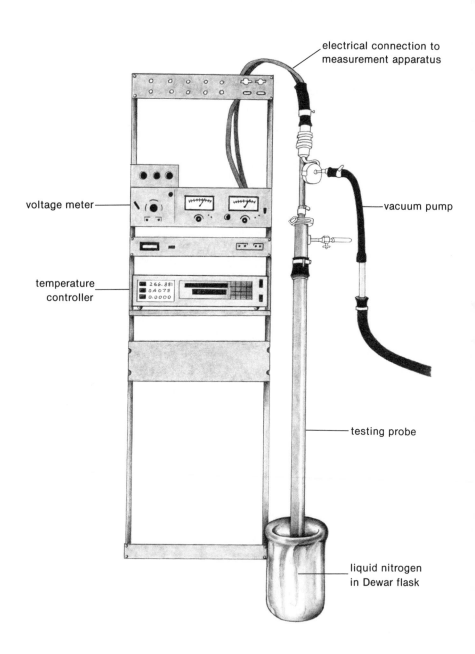

electrical connection to
measurement apparatus

voltage meter

vacuum pump

temperature
controller

testing probe

liquid nitrogen
in Dewar flask

Testing apparatus for superconductive materials

But if superconductivity can be made to work at 225° K., why might it not work at ordinary temperatures that are all about us? That is the dream of scientists right now: to find a substance that will carry electricity without loss, even when it isn't cooled at all, or, at worst, simply when it is air-conditioned as we air-condition our homes.

Of course, scientists can't explain how such high-temperature superconductivity works. Bardeen's explanation for ordinary superconductivity may not fit this new kind. But explanations can wait, if only we can make good use of the discovery.

There is a more practical catch, though. Electricity is conducted along wires and films, for the most part. Wires and films are tough and can bend without breaking. Ceramics are brittle materials. It isn't easy to form wires or films of them. However, scientists are already working on the problem, and there seems to be hope that it may be solved in a reasonable time.

What advantages will high-temperature superconductivity have for all of us? Billions of dollars will be saved in conducting electricity over long distances, but that isn't all.

Because of the loss of electricity while it is being transferred from place to place, generators are placed near cities where the electricity must be used. With high-temperature superconductivity, it would be possible to put the generators far away from cities without losing electricity.

This is particularly important for nuclear power plants. Many people are nervous about having such plants near cities, in case of nuclear accidents. With high-temperature superconductivity, nuclear power plants can be put in isolated desert areas without loss.

Someday we hope to have solar energy, making use of special devices that can turn the energy of sunlight into electricity. Such devices would have to be placed in desert areas, because that is where one finds a great deal of sunshine. Ordinarily such locations would mean long-distance transfer of electricity, with much loss and expense, but with high-temperature superconductivity this loss will not occur.

Nowadays it is very hard to store electricity for future use. Electricity, racing through wires, is quickly lost through resistance. This means that generators must simply produce a lot of electricity when a lot is needed, and less when less is needed. It is hard to work this out, and sudden unexpected surges of electricity use put a great strain on the generating equipment.

With high-temperature superconductivity, however, the electricity can be sent round and round circuits without any loss. In that case, electricity can be stored in circuits during periods of low use, and then be sent as needed into other circuits during periods of high use. This would be another source of improved efficiency.

High-temperature superconductivity would mean a great deal for computers. Computers have been

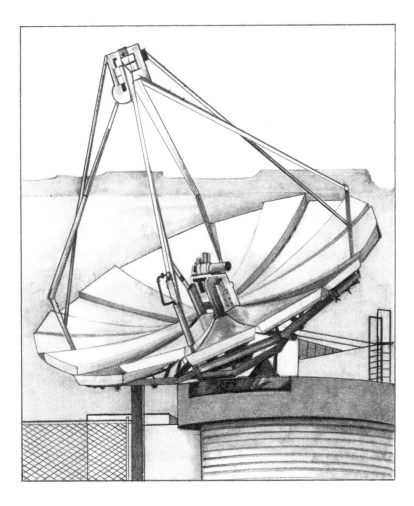

Solar energy device

made smaller and smaller. Now there are tiny chips onto which many wires and electric circuits are crowded. If the chips are made any smaller, and the circuits squeezed in more tightly, much electricity will be changed to heat in the small space. Chips will melt. With high-temperature superconductivity no heat will be produced, and chips can be made even smaller and more crowded. Computers will become smaller, faster, cheaper, and capable of doing far more than they do now.

People have long talked about the possibility of placing trains or other vehicles on rails that carry a strong electric current. This current would produce a powerful magnetic field that could push against the vehicle and lift it a fraction of an inch above the rail. The vehicle would then move without making contact. There would be practically no friction, or the drag effect it causes.

Such vehicles might reach speeds of up to 300 miles per hour and do it so smoothly that people would find it hard to tell they were moving. It would take high-temperature superconductivity to make the use of all that electric current practical. If we lose current through resistance, such magnetic vehicles might be too expensive.

Finally, scientists are trying to work out new ways of getting nuclear energy. Instead of the nuclear *fission* (breaking large atoms in two) that we use now, we might use nuclear *fusion* (forcing small atoms together). Nuclear fusion could produce much more energy than nuclear fission can and be safer, too.

Magnetically levitated train
using superconductive magnets

The trouble is, though, that in order to hold the small atoms in place while they are being forced together, very strong magnetic fields must be used. Again, with high-temperature superconductivity, such magnetic fields can be made stronger and less expensive. So far, scientists have worked toward nuclear fusion energy for thirty years without making it practical. Perhaps, with high-temperature superconductivity, success will come. Then humanity will have a new source of energy that, like solar energy, will never run out.

It isn't surprising that the scientists who first detected high-temperature superconductivity received Nobel prizes in 1987. They were K. Alex Müller of Switzerland and J. Georg Bednorz of West Germany.

And all this started because scientists were curious about absolute zero, tried to find out how close they could get to it, and learned how materials behave at such low temperatures.

Index